PETITION

PETITION

BRUCE SCHAFFER

Petition: A formal written request, signed by many people, appealing to authority with respect to a particular cause.

In a statement: To express the particular of in speech or writing.

Job title information hand guide. How to become a actor in the appearance of: conspirator Brigadier General Dr. lieutenant Bruce Raymone Schaffer DOB: 08/08/1981. Debut Coming soon.

Word count: 6,713.

This is a memoir Shakespeare biography manuscript.

Paranoia productions. Acute entertainment. The name of this motion picture subject is "Psych".

Paranoia productions is the Diagnosis: paranoia Schezoaphective Bypolar type. Acute entertainment is the symptoms. "as needed" PRN. Described Short-term, contract, part-time, or fill-in work by a nurse or allied health professional. Forced medication.

How can you be in the likeness of people that were born in the 1800's and they are all dead? And Bruce Raymone Schaffer is born 08/08/1981 in the 21st century? If i say I'm one of them then how come I'm not dead? When I'm still alive 10/22/2019 etc.

Who wrote the declaration of independence: John adams, Benjamin Franklin, Thomas Jefferson, Roger Sherman, and Robert Livingston. Fifty six members of congress signed it. July 4, 1776 The declaration of independence said "we are dead". When in the course of human events it becomes necessary for one people to dissolve the political bands which have connected them with another and to assume among the powers of the earth the seperate and equal station to which the laws of nature and of nature's god entitled them a decent respect to the opinions of mankind, requires that they should declare the causes which impel them to the separation. And for the support of this declaration with a firm reliance on the protection of divine Providence we mutually pledge to each other our lives our fourtunes and our sacred honor.

Germanies revolutionary Movement, having taken part. During the American civil war. Fredericksburg December 1862. Capture $100,000 reward.

Staring author Bruce Raymone Schaffer initials: B S. (Brown spot). a Brown Spot on the right side of the eye on the right side of the face. DOB: 08/08/1981.

PETITION

I CAN SEE ME NOW, AND THEIR I WAS.

May 14, 1906 our country wrong or right. when right to be kept right. When wrong to be put right. I shurz carl statesman reformer and a union army general in the civil war.

Bruce Schaffer is in the appearance of Shurz carl a senator from Missouri. Was born in liblar near colongue Germany march 2, 1829. Educated at the gymnasium of colongue and the university of Bonn. Was involved in radical politics. In germanies revolutionary movement, having taken part. I was later also forced to flee to Switzerland. I Shurz carl immigrated to the united states in 1855. I Shurz carl and my wife bought a farm on Watertown Wisconsin. Margarethe shurz my wife was the founder of the first kindergarten in America. A strong support of universal suffrage shurz had wrote our idol's resemble the stars which aluminates the night no one will ever be able to touch them but the men who like the saliors on the ocean that take them for guides will undoubtedly reach their goals. So I Bruce Schaffer, shurz carl, one of the men who like the sailors on the ocean took Edwin as Booth for a guide to undoubtedly reach my goals at the age of 17 to perform a play for Lincoln.

And I Booth was to perform a play for Lincoln and Lincoln was suppose to show up to the play. And when Lincoln was to show up to the play I booth and the confederacy were to kidnap Lincoln to make Lincoln recognize the union. But Lincoln never showed up to see the play. So thats when the kidnapping Turned into assassination.

And judge , Michael Kauffman said, that I booth proposed kidnapping Lincoln to my friends Arnold and o'laughlin sometime in August 1864. But nora titone has I booth joining my family at a summer cottage on long island sound on August 1. Throttling john sleeper clarke in a train to Philadelphia most likely on August 7. Then returning to newyork and spending the rest of august in bed with arresapeles. Unless I booth went from Philadelphia to Baltimore where I met Arnold and o'laughlin then took sick and went quickly back to newyork either Kauffman, titone, or booth have their chronology wrong can anyone shed light on this.

In a screen play Bruce Schaffer had an appearance as the new brother Edwin as the leading man John Wilkes Booth. John Wilkes booth sister Asia said john wilkes booth you will never be as good of an actor as your father brutus booth. I didn't want to rival my brother edwin. It was rough and an embarrassment. But a pseudonym helped me get over that. So thats when I Bruce Schaffer as shurz carl a strong support of universal suffrage took edwin as a guide to undoubtedly reach my goals as a actor to act and considered it and begin to cut my teeth under a different name and begin to go by the name of J B Wilkes.

In 1862 Booth made his newyork debut, this time as the lead in richard 111. When describing his natural inclination of the role, I booth tellingly expressed his cedo with the declaration, I am determined to be a villain. Playing the role as John wilkes Booth one mid day in august 1855 john wilkes Booth rode up to tudor hall looking jubilant. It was my first professional stage appearance and i was flushed with excitement. Without telling any one I signed up to play a role at charles street theatre in Baltimore. John sleeper clarke in the stock company there had recommended I to his friend henry c jarrett and henry c jarrett cast I as richmond in a popular adaptation of richard 111.

I John Wilkes booth first performance was a big step but hardly an auspicious beginning. I did not actually perform all of Richard 111- just the battle scene. More over the charles street theatre was not Baltimore' s finest playhouse. It kept no consistent stock company, and rarely featured exceptional talent. It was the last week of a slow summer season and manager jarrett was doing little more than keeping the place open. Jarrett seemed to be using his theatre to audition new actors for the Baltimore Museum which he also ran one block away. Mary was not happy. She thought that her son had been rushed into the business by clarke who was eager to cash in on the booths name. In fact the Baltimore sun' s announcement made it obvious. Mr. John wilkes booth farewell benefit!

thats when I moved to Bal Air, Maryland in my father's house on the road to Churchville. My father's house for rent to a good tenant if immediate application is made. 180 acres of land, 80 which is arable. Address. John wilkes booth Baltimore MD. Sangamon county jail 1 sheriff's plaza, Springfield, IL 62701.

Thats where I Booth had taken a job at the arch street theatre in Philadelphia. The pay was barely adequate, but eight dollors a week, it was twice as much as some of the other were getting. Mary ann, rosalie, and asia would follow me to the quaker city. Joseph would come along, too, at least for a while.

Their, I was A leading member of the republican party. In 1860 I shurz carl campaign for president Lincoln in Illinois, Indiana, Missouri, Ohio, Pennsylvania, and Wisconsin. President Lincoln appointed I shurz as U.S. Envoy to Spain.

I was An active campaigner against slavery and on the outbreak of American join forces of the union army. I also helped recuit germans living in newyork before being asked to negotiate for the European government on the behalf of Abraham Lincoln.

Playing the role as Shurz Carl I served under general John Fremont the commander of the Department of the West. What I was Soon after, before being giving the ranking of brigadier General and placed in command of the third division of the army of

Virginia. I was Soon after, commander of the Department of the west. All of the money of the $100,000 reward in $2 dollar bills replaced with $100.00 dollar bills for the capture of any conspirator of booth.

In that time I Shurz Carl also commanded the third division of the army of the potomac. I also took part in the battles at bullrun and Fredericksburg December 1862. I was promoted to the ranking of major general replacing friend and fellow Franz sigel. I also took part in the battles at chancellorsville and Gettysburg. Before being giving the ranking of brigadier General and placed in command of the third division of the army of the cumberland.

After leaving office. To while hiding, Harold and I, to capture any conspirator. I Shurz Carl returned to journalism becoming a managing editor for the newyork evening post. I also wrote for Harper's weekly "the nations" and had several books published including the lifc's of Henry clay and Abraham Lincoln. I died may 14, 1906.

Before I wrote and published several books including the lifes of, how I have always been in favor of a healthy Americanization. but this doesn't mean a complete disadvowel of our german heritage. It means that our character should take on the best of that which is American and combine it with the best of that which is german. By doing so we can best serve the American people and their civilizations. A healthy americanization of people who is the president, who is the patient, that is unable to testify Taking their psych medicine. The liquid poison.

 That was in sangamon county jail 1 sheriff's plaza, Springfield, IL 62701 where I had visited the places where the surgeant were at work at bullrun I had seen only a very small scall of what I was now to behold. At Gettysburg the wounded, many thousands of them were carried to farm steds behind our lines. The houses, the sheds, and the open barn yards were crowded with moaning a welling human beings. And the unceasing procession of stretchers and ambulances were coming in from all side's to augment the number of sufferers.

Who were placed in the medical chart that I J B Wilkes in an appearance as Sherman who believed in maneuvering received a telegraphic message from secretary Stanton containing the announcement of the assassination of President Lincoln. The terrible news was kept a secret from our troops to be revealed to them in general order the next day. I well remember the effect the announcement had upon them. The camps which for two days had been fairly resounding with jubilation over the advent of peace suddenly fell into a gloomy stillness. The soldiers admired their great generals but there good father Abraham they loved. The soldiers couldn't believe it a medical chart of a telegraphic message containing the announcement of the assassination of President Lincoln. The patient taking the liquid poison.

From the legislature branch: powers here-in granted in a united states congress. Which shall consist of a senate and a house of representatives. Congress has the power to make the united states laws. To impeach an official of the government meaning charging him with treason, bribery, other high crimes or misdemeanors the house of representatives serves as the prosecutor brining specific charges against the individual. And the senate serves as the judge and the jury residing the proceedings making the legal decisions. The result of impeachment is removal from office. No future government position . 2/3rds majority to convict.

but in fact, john wilkes booth followed the standared path for all actors of his day At Sangamon county jail 1 sheriff's plaza, Springfield, IL 62701, private study, apprenticeship, and stock experience. Formal training did not yet exist, and the best one could hope for was a bit of coaching and advice from seasoned professionals. I John wilkes booth had three of those Lincolns living right at home. At sangamon county jail 1 sheriff's plaza, Springfield, IL 62701. Nor did I john wilkes booth neglect my voice, subject of many a discussion at the arch.

It is saying a great deal that I booth was a much handsomer man than my brother Edwin. I possessed a voice very much like my brother ' s melodies, sweet, full, and strong, and was like him a consummate elocutionist. John wilkes booth seems to have preserved some measure of anonymity at the arch though insiders surely knew who he was. It probably helped that he was billed as Mr. wilks when there happened to be a stage family of that name working in the city. John shafer & association. INC. Architects & planners 1230 south six street, Springfield, illinois 62703.

Where I john wilkes booth had grown up to be a handsome young man in that town with wavy, dark hair, and lustrous eyes that were a Booths trademark. And of course there was raw talent. Alfriend thought that although I john wilkes was still in training my natural ability was beyond question. I Booth as he recalled had a knack for making friends. I knew all of the best men and many of the finest women. I had inherited an air of confidence and an easy faculty for social success. I always left a warm and pleasing impression. With men I dignified and bore myself with insouciant care and grace. To women I was a man of irresistible fascination with a peculiar halo of romance with which I invested myself and which the ardent imagination of women amplified. John wilkes booth sex appeal has for some reason drawn far more attention than it deserves. Certainly many women sought his companionship. They threw themselves foolishly at me and we have no reason to suspect that I made a habit of turning them away. But in a breathtaking stretch of logic George Alfred Townsend tied I Booth's worthless moral nature to my poor acting. This in turn I opined gave rise to a professional despair that led I to kill the president. I Booth said that Townsend was distracted by that careless class of women who are always looking out for aquaintances with actors and he indulged to much in frivolous escapades at the exspense of his studies. A more recent author went a step futher suggesting that I Booth shot the president who is the patient while suffering from the mental effects of tertiary syphilis. that was just he say she say. nobody really knows.

Like many other actors the booths had long been a political. But the war had made them very republican. They were strong unionist except for john wilkes who's sympathies lay with the south. At one point john and even to some extent his sister Asia had aligned themselves with the know nothing party. During the war his views aligned much better with the democrates. So I declared War. It led me to assassinate the president who is the patient who are unable to testify that take psych medicine the liquid poison.

Shit In Philadelphia it had a rich dramatic history. It was home to Edwin forrest and Charlotte cushman and to a host of up-and-coming new talent. As I booth began my work at the arch, I struck up a friendship with john McCullough, a fellow neophyte from the so call boothinians dramatic society, the largest of the city's theatrical clubs. A native of blakes, londonderry, McCullough was five years older than booth. A man of little education, he had immigrated to Philadelphia in 1849 to escape the famine in his native land. He was working in a chair factory when a fellow worker gave him a book of Shakespeare's plays. McCullough was hooked, and join the boothinians right away. When manager wheatley offered him four dollars a week for the smallest of roles, like acting as a conspirator, he exccepted without hesitation, giving up a job that paid more than twice that much. I booth and McCullough feared. We began to carry a gun and wear a bullet proof vest and became the marshall. And we used drubbing from lee to get it. McCullough and I had been granted because our campaign believed in hammering and hammering without loosing sight of Sherman campaign that believed in maneuvering.

In the opinion of many competent persons I was the ablist commander of them all. I remember a remarkable utterances of his when we were speaking of grants campaign. Their was a differents sherman said between grant and my way of looking at things. Grant never care a damb about what was going on behind enemy lines but it often scared me like the devil. I admitted and justly so that some of grants successes were owing to this very fact but also some of my conspicuous failures. I Grant believed in hammering. I Sherman in maneuvering. It had been a habit of the generals army of the potomac to cross the rapahanock to get their drubbing from lee. Then promptly to retreat and recross the rapahanock again in retreat. I sturdy went on hammering and hammering and with my vastly superior resources finally hammered lee's army to pieces. But with the most dreadful sacrifice of life on my own part. Now comparing grants campaign for the taking of richmond with Sherman campaign for the taking of atlanta without loosing sight of any of the differences of their respective situations we may well arrive at the conclussion that Sherman was the superior strategies and greater general.

Thats when booth lost his job at the marshall, but on hearing the good news, a contingent of grays marched on the theater and pleaded to have him reinstated. Though George kunkel gave me my job back, I booth had lost my enthusiasm for acting. The excitement of recent Events had made me think once more of a career in uniform. The idea terrified my mother, but as asia said, military service was probably her brothers dearest ambition. His good friend jesse wharton had been commissioned in the army, and now I john wilkes poundered the idea of following him into the ranks. In, the end, though, he chose to continue acting. Audiences loved him, and critical notice was uniformly good. When the season opened, he would return to the stage with top billing.

in may 1860 when Lincoln was nominated to be the republican candidate for president who is the patient. That summer when booth was in new york to attend a wedding of Edwin and mary devilin he got in touch with Matthew w. Canning, Jr., a Philadelphia lawyer and part owner of some play houses in the south. Canning had put together a touring company for the coming season , and on I edwins recommendation, I signed I john wilkes as it's leading man. After three years of stock acting I john wilkes booth was about to become a star. Thats when I had received a necklace with a star on it that represented that I were a marshall who was involved in the underground and the work demanded travel.

Shit the whole structure was to be living incarnations of this idea. Should i point out to you the consequences of a deviation from this principal. Look at the slaves states. This is a class of men who are deprived of their natural rights. But this isn't the only deplurable feature of that peculiar organization of society. Equally deplurable is it that theirs another class of men who keeps the former in subject. That their are slaves is bad but what that is worse is that their are masters. Are not masters free men no sir, where is the liberty of the speech. Where is the liberty of the press. Where is the man amonst them who dare to advocate openly principals not in strict accordance with the ruling systems. They speak of a republican form of government. They speak of a democracy. By, But the despotic spirit of slavery and mastership combine that pervades the whole political life like a liquid poison. If you want to be free their is only but one way it is to guarantee an equally full measure of liberty to all of your neighbors. Mc-Clellan was to late. He voted no to cross the potomac and richmond To give the president who is the patient a shot of 156 milligrams of invega the liquid poison to be able to be placed with a burnsied on our hippa by taking advantage of the president who is the patient who is a people unable to testify, to be able to have a burnside a gun.

when McClellan at last had crossed the potomac and richmond. The president removed him from his command and put general Burnside the gun in his place. Burnside was my gun on my hippa. The selection for Burnside for so great a responsibility was not a happy one. I was a very patriotic man whose heart was in my work. Because of my gun, my Burnside on my hippa it's sincerity, frankness and am I ability of manner made every body like me but I was not a great general and I felt myself, my bullet proof vest, that the task to which I had been assign was to heavy for my shoulders. The complaint against McClellan having being his slowness to act. Burnside resolved to act at once and the plan of campaign it conceived were to cross the rapahanock, meaning give the president who is the patient a shot of the liquid poison, at fredericksburgh and thence to operate upon Richmond. And began to chart in the medical chart the liquid poison.

at least as George atzerodt told it their were lots of reasons why I booth wanted to kill licoln one of them was simply that he thought a group of plotters from new york would try to do it and he wanted to beat them to the punch. He really like being top dog..

Mean while. The other conspirator like I who served the south like I, of the sincerity, frankness, and am I ability of manner that made every body like them was presently having a play, on the set in sangamon county jail 1 sheriff's plaza, Springfield, IL 62701. Just before we was about to give the president a shot of invega the liquid poison and McCullough was showing off with my fellow co-workers joking around in a play. Showing off in front of the president who is the patient before transporting him across the street from Ford's theater at the chester mental health center P.O. Box 0031. The play was our American cousin a popular british comedy from the 1850s. Its humor was derived from the homespun

" Yankeeisms" of asa trenchard a backwoods vermonter and the physical eccentricities of lord dundreary a self important british nobleman. The star was laura keene a london native whose character Florence trenchard believe that her cousin asa (played by actor henry hawk) has just inherited the family fortune. Florence and her british relatives try to stay in asa good grace but find it difficult to overlook his crass country boy manner. It is this culture clash that carries the play. For most of the audience that night however our American cousin was not the main attraction. A notice in that days evening star had announced that president Abraham Lincoln and his wife would attend the performance. Their guest would be ulysses S. Grant lieutenant general of the army victor of the recent war hero of the hour. This suprise reservation had come in that morning and it sent harry clay ford brother of the theartre owner on a mad dash to organize a special program. A patriotic song called " honor to our soldier " was written for the occasion and ford sent notices of it to the evenings star. The marshalls. He even redesigned the evenings playbill to reflect the new Developments. By late afternoon, the reservations were rolling in. A normally dismal night was now showing some promise. By curtain time, at eight o' clock, Ford's theatre had a fairly good house.

By ten-fifteen, our American cousin had progress to the second scene of the third act. Asa trenchard had told a woman name mrs. Mountchessington that he hadn't inherited a fourtune after all , as everyone thought, and the character (played by Helen muzzy) had a change of heart about the marriage she had hope to arrange between asa and her daughter augusta. Asa (to Augusta): you crave affection , you do. Now I've no fortune, but I'm biling over with affections, which I'm ready to pour out to all of you, like apple sass over roasted pork. Mrs. Mountchessington: mr. Trenchard, you will please recollect you are addressing my daughter, and in my presence. Asa: yes, I'm offering her my heart in my hand just as she wants them, with nothing in ' em.

Though lincoln was hidden from view most of the time, he occasionally leaned over the box railing to look down into the audience. That is how Isaac Jacquette, in the dress circle, got his first look at him. It was halfway into the play, and a woman sitting nearby remarked that she had never seen the president before. A man whispered that she might see him now, as he was leaning forward. Everytime he came into view, the president stole the show.

The president's guest seemed to enjoy the play. Miss harris had been the Lincoln's guest here before. Major rathbone, of the 12th u.s. infantry, was not quite so familiar to them. He had commanded a company under burnside his gun at antietam and Fredericksburg.

saloon owner james p. Ferguson on the far side of the first balcony had reconize the man in black as I john wilkes booth.

On april 14, 1865 john wilkes booth was the first person to assassinate an american president who shot and killed Lincoln in his box at fords theatre in washington. At sangamon county jail 1 sheriff's plaza, Springfield, IL 62701. Using a 44 caliber. The liquid poison. A derringer pistol. A easily to council handgun. A 156 milligrams shot of invega injected into the potomac and Richmond. I Booth fired a single shot of invega the liquid poison into Lincoln brain point blank range timed so that that laughing audience would mask the report before jumping on stage and escaping into the night. Braking my leg while jumping on stage and screaming out sinc simper tyrannis. Then briefing my accomplices. Then helped on my horse by Harold and we both riding off into the night.

After that shot Lincoln was transported to the petterson house accross the street from Ford's theatre where he eventually died 7:22 AM April 15, 1865. At: chester mental health center P.O.Box 0031.

They took a special interest in booth's movements around the theatre that day. I had been in and out of ford's all afternoon, they learned, and had made a few trips to the neighborhood restaurant as well. All most everyone on the crew knew me and enjoyed my company. I took them to lunch, bought them drinks, and generally made them feel at ease. I always treated the crew as equals, and not many stars did that. Some of the theater people looked after the horse and ran other errands for I booth as well.

After I booth gave Lincoln the shot of invega the liquid poison in the potomac and Richmond. Leale pulled off the president coat and peeled back his shirt. But even with the shoulders exsposed , he could find no knife wound. Fanning his fingers through the president's hair, at last he found something. On the back of the head a little to the left of the center was a bullet hole. The tissue around it had swelled and a clot had formed in the opening. Leale pulled his hand away and the wound bled. As it did the president who is the patient began to breathe more freely.

After all, how would it look if the great martyr should die in a playhouse-and on good friday, at that? Theatres still carry the stigma of immortality, and nobody wanted abraham Lincoln to take his last breathe in such a place.

Prior when The soldiers who had carried the president who is the patient had left the building, but were not sure where to go. As they made their way through a sea of people, some of the spectators jockeyed for a better look, and some even helped by taking a hold of an arm or a leg. They moved aimlessly into the street, heading toward a row of houses that in recent years had become jammed with boarders. Some of these people stood there now looking out their windows and wondering how they might be of help. An artist named carl r. Bersch sketched the event from his balcony while one of his neighbors took a more active part. Henry safford a young war department clerk stepped out the front door with a candle and called down from the landing bring him in here! To Chester mental health center P.O.Box 0031. Safford was living in a respectable middle class house at 453 tenth street. It was owned by william petterson a German boy tailor who lived there with his wife anna and three of their children. They had alway taken in boarders and the place had been a favorite among actors who liked the convenience of living accross from fords..

In fact , nobody even drew their weapons and though a few men did mack a rush for the back door , for a veriety of reasons they went no further. James S. Knox and E.D. Wray were among those who ran to the stage. Wray made a detour to pick something up off the stage, and others stopped when they heard a woman say they'll get him or they've got him - nobody was sure which. Only a few actually went out the back door , and the only person they found there was a frightened young boy , who said that mr. Booth had struck him over the head with something as he mounted his horse.

A rumor went around that booth had been captured, and cries of hanging him tore through the crowd., That was the first of many such false alarms , and each was followed by louder shouts for revenge. This time , one man stood on the chair and shouted , take out the ladies and hang him here on the spot!

While the men felt embarrassed that I booth had gotten away , the women were simply terrified. It was the coolest, most cold-blooded deed ever heard, read, or dreamed of, wrote Sarah hamlin batchelder. Hours after the shooting sarah was still trying to find the right words for what she had witnessed: it is certainly unnerved me. My own shadow... would have startled me.... This is terrible, awful horrible, nothing can describe the intense feeling of fear & dread of more to come and none can judge in the least degree it's depth and save those who witnessed the horrible scenes.

The confederate soldiers, conspirator, wanted his men to keep a watch out for the horse I booth was riding and fortunately a description was easy to get. "Peanut" barrows had been holding the mare at the time of the shooting. Though he was just a boy he turned out to be an excellent observer. He described the horse to be a little bay mare with a long wavy tail and a heavy fetlock. She had a small flat forehead small nostrils and a very small thin neck that was rather arched. Her mare fell on the left side her ears where small and her rump was sloped. Richards was delighted to have such a wealth of details right down to the temperament which would prove to be important. Booth was a superb horseman and wasn't the least bothered by her disposition. On friday afternoon he had been showing her off to ferguson. See how she starts off? Booth said. And with that he had darted up teenth street.

Confederate prisoners had march right past here en route to the old capital prison. There were more than four hundred of them marching along in their torn and tarnished uniforms with no semblance of bravado and yet with no apparent sense of humiliation. At the time woodward one of boothinians who served the south had felt sorry for those men. Now they came back to mind a different light. Could those same prisoners have been set loose to avenge their lost cause? For Their fellow employee John wilkes Booth? The question preyed on woodward mind and he decided at once to alert the city garrison.

They ran to the Telegraph office together and gobright dictated a quick special to alert the press: washington april 14, President Lincoln was shot to night and is mortally wounded. He promised more details would follow and then hurried over to the scene of the crime. At fords theatre everyone was still in a state of intense excitement. The president had just Been carried out of the building and gobright wanted to see the box before they closed the place down. Holding on to his friend a valuable eyewitness he inspected the actual site of the shooting. They walked right in and surveyed the box to fix the scene of the crime in their minds.

So the dispatch, Secret service agent had helped aid in the escape of john wilkes booth to surrattsville to pick up supply left their earlier. At sangamon county jail 1 sheriff's plaza, Springfield, IL 62701 Then to charlesville at: chester mental health center P.O. Box 0031. to get medical help from Dr. Mudd. That is when I john wilkes booth had an appearance as a debut in Dr. Mudd.

Secretary Stanton, secretary of war stopped by charlesville to speak with Dr. Mudd to ask questions. Secretary Stanton Secretary of war asked did a man with a broken leg come by to you for medical help? Dr. Mudd said no. But if any one said that i fixed their leg that i can't denie the patient. Thats where I john wilkes booth as Dr. Mudd set my leg. That was my excuse to Secretary stanton, My aliby. My set leg was hamlet was announced on october 12, but things did not go as planned. An hour before curtain time, booth was in manager matt canning's hotel room, going through his lines with actor johnny albaugh, when came in looking exhausted. Booth was concerned. Now, you must let me nurse you, he said. You are fagged out. The manager replied that he only wanted to go to sleep. As he lay on the bed, booth noticed a pistol jutting out of canning's back pocket and saw an opportunity to show off. Sliding the weapon out, he carefully took an aim at a mark on the opposite side of the wall. The loud discharge brough the startled canning instantly to his feet. Booth was a supurb marks man, but this time he missed the mark, and he wanted to have another shot at it. Canning on the other hand, just wanted to get his heart back out of his throat. He insisted on having his gun back, but booth would not give it up. They fussed over it, and as they did, booth noticed some rust on the barrel. He got the manager to hold the weapon while he scraped it off with a pocket-knife. The pistol discharged, and the ball struck booth in the thigh, barely missing the femoral artery. It was a serious wound, and one that might have ended his career, if not his life.

Thats when booth As he told his sister asia, he had to keep

moving; it was the only way he could help the cause. I have only an arm to give, he said, but my brains are worth tweenty men, my money worth a hundred. I have free pass everywhere, my profession, my name, is my passport; my knowledge of drugs is valuable, my beloved precious money-oh, never beloved until now!- is the means, one of the means, by which i serve the south. He told her that he was involved in the underground, and the work demanded travel.

anyway, asia said. And then Secretary Stanton, secretary of war said their will be a $ 100,000.00 dollar reward for the capture of john wilkes Booth and any conspirators oF Booth.

March 26th, 1865

thats when mr. Brooks: said to mr. Dr.Booth as business will detain me for a few days in the country, I thought i would send your team back. Mr. Barry will deliver it safely and pay the hire on it. If mr. Dr. Booth my friend should want my horses let him have them, but no one else. If you should want any money on them he will let you have it. I should have like to kept the team for several days, but it is to expensive, especially as i have "woman on the brain" and may be away for a week or so.

Your respectfully
J. Harrison surratt

John surratt must have thought the conspiracy was finished. By leting booth use his horses, "but no one else". He effectively rescinded the privilege from atzerodt, who was still in need of transportation. He could hardly have done the same to booth, since those horses actually belong to him. When mr. Dr. John wilkes booth had gotten the other horse mr. Dr. John wilkes booth had an appearance in a debut as the lieutenant owner of the tobacco barn chester mental health center P.O. Box 0031. Of Dr. John P. Garrett wilkes booth, lieutenant over the 16th newyork calvary. Leading 27 men.

Headed southward while Dr. John P. Garrett wilkes Booth and Harold were hiding Dr. John P. Garrett wilkes Booth lieutenant over the sixteenth new york Calvary with sergeant Boston, Dr. lieutenant john P. Garrett wilkes Booth led 27 men on the hunt for john wilkes booth.

The conspirator Harold and booth arrived at garretts house. Garrett also had a tobacco barn behind his house. At: chester mental health center. P.O. Box 0031 Booth introduced himself as James Boyd to Garrett, and Garrett took harold and James boyd politeness and let them sleep in his tobacco barn for the night. Garrett who had owned the tobacco barn told the where abouts of James Boyd and Harold to secretary Stanton, secretary of war that Harold and James boyd are hiding in my tobacco barn. Harold and booth was found hiding in a barn near port royal virginia. Harold surrendered. Booth refused to come out of the barn so it was set on fire. In the ensuing chaos a soldier shot and killed booth. After a two week man hunt Federal troops cornered booth in a barn in maryland where a union soldier shot him in the neck. Booth died two hours later. Harold and james boyd as a conspirator as booth who also served the south as one of the helped recuits living in newyork, had been tracked down. By Dr. Lieutenant john P. Garrett wilkes booth, then sergeant Boston piped booths in a knot whole in the planks and shot booth in the neck. The tobacco barn went up in flames. James boyd was grabbed out of the barn and laid on Garrett porch in a paralyzed state. James boyd as booth died three hour later. The body of booth was autopsied and released to the family.

At: Helping Hands 1023 E. Washington st, springfield, IL 62703.

Album cover: the left side of the front of Jay-Z face as james boyd attached to the right side of the front of Bruce Raymone Schaffer face. The name of the album: J album. J Meaning: Jay-Z. Meaning: Jail album. Bruce Raymone Schaffer rapper name: Capture. AKA: $100,Bands.

Acknowledgements

[1600-7681-225S]
Appellate Courts
First District
160 N. La Salle Street,
Suite 91400, Chicago, IL
60601

[1600-7681-225S]
Appellate Courts
Second District
Appellate Court Building
55 Symphony Way
Elgin, IL 60120

[1600-7681-225S]
Appellate Courts
Third District
1004 Columbus Street,
Ottawa, IL 61350

[1600-7681-225S]
Appellate Courts
Fourth District
201 W. Monroe Street,
P.O. Box 19206, Springfield,
IL 62794

[1600-7681-225S]
Appellate Courts
Fifth District
14th & Main Streets
P.O. Box 867,
Mount Vernon, IL
62864-0018

[1600-7681-225S]
Appellate Courts
Supreme Court of Illinois
Supreme Court Building
200 E. Capital Ave, Spring-
field, IL 62701

What do I do with letters I receive?
Subpoena a person the witnesses so summoned shall be paid a
fee for the mileage and the same as the witnesses shall be paid
a fee that is in the circuit court. How do I request a revocation
hearing? How do I file my Petition?

[1600-7681-225S]
Appellate Courts
Chairman
Illinois Prisoner Review Board
319 East Madison Street, Suite R
Springfield, IL 62701

What are the filing requirements?

[1600-7681-225S]
Appellate Courts
Cook County State's Attorney
Room 11D38, 2650 South California Avenue,
Chicago, IL 60608

How do I request a governor's hearing?

[1600-7681-225S]
Appellate Courts
Office of the Governor, Extradition Affairs
124 E. Adams, Room 102, P.O. Box 19461,
Springfield, IL 62794-9461

How do I get a witness or representation
For immigration situations?

[1600-7681-225S]
Appellate Courts
Legal Assistance Foundation of Chicago
343 S. Dearborn, Suite 700, Chicago, IL 60604

I lost in the District Court, may I appeal? Yes. Appeals are governed by the Federal Rule of Appellate procedure and the Seventh Circuit practice rules. Notice of appeals and the Civil Rights Act Petition are within 30 day, and within 60 days if you are (suing the United States Marshals).

[Fed.R.App.P.4(2).]. The appeal must have a caption, title, designation. Must be signed by you or your attorney. Must use full address. Certificate, addressed:

> [1600-7681-225S]
> Appellate Courts
> Judges of the Circuit Court of Appeals
> For the Seventh Circuit
> 219 South Dearborn Street,
> Chicago, IL 60604